Ron...

Medieval

Tudor

Stuart

Puritan

William and Mary

Georgian

Regency

Early Victorian

Late Victorian

Edwardian motorist

Series 601

Here is a fascinating book to show you what people have worn from the days of Stone Age skins to the modern mass-produced clothes.

The well-written text and superb colour illustrations add interest to history, and help towards a greater understanding of the past.

CLOTHES
and COSTUME

by Richard Bowood
with illustrations by
Robert Ayton

Publishers: Wills & Hepworth Ltd., Loughborough
First published 1964　　　©　　　*Printed in England*

Furs and Skins

Why do we wear clothes? The main reason is, of course, to keep warm and dry. But that is not all. If you went to school one morning with nothing but a bear skin wrapped round you, you would be beautifully warm. But you would cause a sensation in the streets and you would doubtless be sent home at once to dress properly.

We wear the same kind of clothes as everyone else; we follow the fashion. The fashion in clothes is always changing, and finding out what people wore at different times in history is very interesting. It is also very useful. If you are reading history, say the story of the Norman invasion of 1066, King Henry V at Agincourt in 1415, or Guy Fawkes in 1605, you can understand it much better if you know what the people at that time looked like. The story of clothes helps you to understand the past.

People who live in hot countries do not have to bother much about clothes to keep them warm. But in Britain it can never have been comfortable going about without any clothes, except sometimes in the Summer. Clothes were essential. The first clothes worn by the earliest people in Britain must have been the furs and skins of the animals they killed for food.

Clothes Made of Cloth

Skins and furs went out of use when people found out how to spin, weave and make cloth. They learned to draw out and twist (or *spin*) short lengths of wool or vegetable fibre such as flax, and to make it into continuous thread. This thread they *wove* into cloth by interlacing it closely on a loom.

From pictures and carvings we know the kind of clothes they wore 7,000 years ago in Babylon, Egypt and Assyria. But we have no evidence of when the first woven clothes were worn in Britain.

The earliest proof we have of clothes worn in our part of Europe comes from some actual garments found in Denmark. They were preserved in peat bogs for more than 2,500 years.

The picture shows what people probably wore in Britain about 500 B.C., and is based on the discoveries made in Denmark. The girl has a simple linen tunic. The man has a woollen cloak over his tunic, and wears a 'Phrygian' cap. Both wear sandals, similar to the sandals we wear. They were sensible clothes, and were probably dyed to give a variety of colours.

The Romans

Julius Cæsar invaded Britain in the years 55 and 54 B.C., but the country was not finally conquered and made part of the Roman Empire until a hundred years later. By A.D. 78, there were permanent Roman garrisons in Britain. Roman law, Roman customs, Roman buildings, Roman roads and Roman civilisation gave Britain a completely Roman way of life which lasted for 350 years. Clothes, like everything else, became Roman.

The picture shows a scene in the Romano-British days. A Roman officer has called on a magistrate in his villa. The magistrate, wearing the toga of his rank, is drinking wine with his guest. His wife, dressed as a noble lady, is helping him to entertain. The lady's woman-slave is in attendance.

We have a number of ruins of these beautifully built Roman villas in Britain, and although very few clothes have lasted, we have pictures and models. Plenty of the jewellery, weapons and coins, especially coins, have come down to us. We do know that the material of the clothes was very good, and that the people of the Romano-British period were well dressed.

Saxons and Normans

When William of Normandy defeated Harold of England in 1066, the Normans settled and later mingled with the Anglo-Saxon race. The event made but little difference to clothes, because Harold's and William's people wore much the same. The only noticeable difference was that the Normans had their hair cut shorter.

Soldiers wore chain mail and pointed helmets with a bar of steel to protect the nose and the front of the face. Civilian dress was the tunic, often with a pattern at the edge. The leg coverings were usually bound with leather thongs.

Ladies wore long gowns, sometimes with pretty girdles. Light blue, red and green were the fashionable colours. Cloaks, fastened with a cord at the neck, were worn by men and women. Rich people had fur-lined cloaks for cold weather.

The picture shows the lord of the manor as he prepares to ride out to join the king. He is wearing chain-mail, with a strong belt to hold his mighty two-handed sword. The man-at-arms is holding his lord's helmet.

Medieval—The Court

The picture shows a scene at Court in the fourteenth century, perhaps about the year 1360. Rich people wore very bright clothes and fashions were extravagant. Ladies wore tall pointed hats and sometimes a wimple— a white cloth which covered the neck. The older lady is wearing one.

Sometimes men wore particoloured clothes, one side one colour, the other side another, like the man speaking to the king at the high table. The part-coloured clothes continued through later centuries as the traditional dress of the jester.

The man in the front of the picture wears very wide sleeves, which are 'dagged' or cut. He has rather long hair and such very long toes to his shoes that they have to be fastened to his legs with thin chains.

There were many fashions in the mediæval period, but only among the well-to-do, for clothes were very expensive. There were strict laws about dress; ermine could only be worn by royalty and the nobility, and only knights and people of higher rank were allowed to wear cloth of gold. Even the length of the pointed shoes was regulated by law, allowing different lengths for nobility, gentlemen and commoners.

Medieval—The Common People

Poorer people wore a simple costume, more sensible and less ornamental. They had to work, and as the work did not change, so the fashion remained the same.

The man in the picture is setting off to market with his pack-horse, the best way of carrying things when roads were bad. He wears a tunic with long, narrow sleeves. The wide, fancy 'dagged' sleeves were only worn by rich people who had no need to work. His cloth hose fit closely and his boots are home-made from soft leather. His purse is on his belt.

He wears a hood with a very long point, called a 'liripipe'. This was not just fashion; it served a useful purpose. On a cold day he could wrap it round his neck like a scarf.

The woman is going visiting, riding side-saddle. She wears a long gown, but with tighter sleeves than wealthy ladies. She has a mantle over the gown, and a white wimple under her sensible hat.

The boy tending sheep wears a smaller version of his father's clothes; a tunic, cloth hose, home-made shoes and a hood with a wide collar. On warm days the hood could be thrown back off the head.

Medieval—Armour

The knight is riding out from his castle. He has been summoned by his overlord to fight in the Civil War called the Wars of the Roses. This could be any time between 1455 and 1471, or perhaps he is riding to fight on Bosworth Field in 1485. All the great Barons had their own knights, men-at-arms, archers and footsoldiers. Each knight, when summoned, led his own men-at-arms and foot-soldiers. Either·they followed the King to fight in France, or their own Baron if there was war at home.

The armour had changed from the chain mail of the Norman days to beautifully made and very handsome plate armour. It was a good protection against arrow, sword or lance, but it was not very comfortable. It was so heavy that very big and strong horses had to be used to carry the knight, and if a man in full armour was unhorsed he was extremely clumsy. If he was knocked over he was almost helpless.

The knight in the picture wears a linen surcoat emblazoned with his coat of arms. His vizor is up, but it will be dropped to cover his face when.he goes into action. Then he can only see out of a slit, like the commander of a modern tank. His horse also wears armour and a surcoat, the latter being sometimes worn over the armour.

The Tudor Period

Henry Tudor defeated King Richard III at Bosworth in 1485 and became King Henry VII. England was ruled by the Tudors for a hundred and twenty years, and with them came a new Age. The knight on the previous page belonged to the 'Age of Chivalry', but this now ended. Many things changed—including clothes.

Men wore broad-shouldered doublets, puffed sleeves, short cloaks, square-toed shoes and flat hats with a gay feather. Clothes were rich, colourful and splendid.

Ladies wore the 'gable hood' on their heads, pointed in front like a little roof with a black cloth at the back. Men and women wore fur on their cloaks, and rich men wore a gold chain. Daggers were worn at the belt, and were used at the table, and every gentleman wore a sword. Children, as always until the last century, wore small versions of their parents' clothes, and small babies were bandaged up in what must have been a most uncomfortable manner.

Queen Elizabeth I—The Court

Although Queen Elizabeth I (1558—1603) was a Tudor, her reign was so notable that it has its own name—The Elizabethan Age. Dress had been splendid during the reign of her father, Henry VIII, but now it became gorgeous—for the rich.

New silks and velvets were brought in from France and Italy, and new fashions came with them. Starch came into use to stiffen linen and this led to the ruff, a stiff frilled collar which was a feature of Elizabethan dress. Worn by men and women, ruffs became larger and more complicated as the years passed.

Men's doublets were padded in front, and they wore short padded 'trunk hose', or breeches, long stockings and very fine short cloaks. Ladies wore the 'farthingale', a fat roll worn round the hips, to make the skirt stand out and show the beautiful embroidery to full effect.

In the picture Queen Elizabeth is receiving a gentleman at Court. We have a number of magnificent paintings of the Queen in her gorgeous clothes. Notice the pearls and jewels she is wearing. The Secretary of State, with the paper, wears rich but sober clothes.

An Elizabethan Merchant

The splendid clothes on the previous page belong to the grand world of the Court. But in Queen Elizabeth's reign good clothes were worn by other classes as well, and as always the fashion set by the rich was followed by the others. Ruffs, most carefully starched and ironed, were worn by everyone with any claim to respectability.

In the picture, a London merchant and his wife have gone on board a ship which has just come back from a voyage to the New World, which we now call America. The Captain is showing the merchant some of the treasure he has brought back; it was probably taken from a Spanish ship after an exciting sea-fight on the Spanish Main.

The merchant's gown is trimmed with fur and his gold chain shows his wealth. His young apprentice is doubtless dreaming of one day going on a voyage as a merchant adventurer. The merchant's wife is wearing a ruff and a full skirt, and a smart hat with a feather. Her little girl is wearing a smaller version of the same clothes. The ship's captain wears a leather doublet.

The Cavaliers

After Queen Elizabeth I, the last of the Tudors, came the Stuart Kings, and a change in clothes and fashion. The stiff ruff gradually gave place to a wide turned down collar, sometimes edged with lace and sometimes all lace. The short, full trunk hose were replaced by knee-length breeches. Men wore lace frills at wrists and knees. Wide brimmed and very elegant hats had fine feathers. Men wore their hair long, curling to the shoulder. With their long hair, curly-brimmed hats, feathers and lace, the Stuart men were very elegant indeed. They wore high, soft leather boots and very finely made swords.

All the stiffness and padding went from women's clothes, and they wore very graceful dresses with lace collars and cuffs. Hair was done up at the back into a bun and allowed to fall in curls on each side of the face. Wide brimmed hats with feathers were worn by ladies, too, like the men, The Stuart ladies were very beautifully dressed—if they could afford it.

When men wore shoes, they, like the women, had elegant ones, often with red heels. It was an easy, charming kind of dress, in very good taste.

The Puritans

England was bitterly divided in the seventeenth century by the Civil War between King Charles I and his Parliament. In 1649 the King was executed and Parliament, under Oliver Cromwell, ruled until 1660 when King Charles II returned from exile. In the Civil War, the King's men were called Cavaliers, the Parliament men were the Puritans.

The Puritans marked their opposition to the Cavaliers by dressing quietly; in contrast to the lace, feathers and splendour of the Royalists. They wore plain clothes of sober black, grey, fawn or brown. Their wide collars had no lace, though sometimes they did allow themselves a modest feather in their high-crowned hats.

Ladies wore plain clothes too, with wide, white collars and little, white caps. This fashion was often most becoming, for the simplicity of line and design provided a charming setting for a pretty face.

The Puritans were devout and believed in living simple and good lives, and the Bible was their constant guide. In the picture a Puritan has been reading the family Bible before a meal.

William and Mary

With the restoration of King Charles II to the throne in 1660, the Puritan simplicity of dress was ended, and clothes were once again rich and colourful.

When William and Mary became King and Queen in 1688, a new reign again brought new fashions.

The change in dress was slight but there was one important development, the 'periwig' worn by men. This was an enormous, and a very expensive wig which fell in heavy curls to the shoulders. Rich clothes, rich colours, and fine manners brought elegance and a rather theatrical style.

Ladies' clothes changed in many details, the most important being the 'frontage'. This was a tall linen or lace arrangement on wires fixed to the front of a small cap.

The lady in the picture is wearing a 'frontage'. She has a 'manteau', or overskirt pulled back and bunched up behind to show her pretty underskirt. The milkmaid wears laced bodice and a straw hat.

The gentleman's coat is richly worked and has a full skirt. It is worn unbuttoned to show his beautifully embroidered waistcoat. His 'tricorne', or three-cornered, hat is typical of the period. His cravat is trimmed with lace, and his shoes would have handsome silver buckles.

Georgian

The Georgian period began when King George I came to the throne in 1714, and continued through the reigns of George II and George III until about 1811. Many changes of fashion took place in this long period. At first a very large periwig was worn by men but this gradually gave way to a smaller, neater wig, and then the pig-tail came into fashion. This was a short tail of natural hair at the back, tied with a neat bow of ribbon. The lace cravat, as worn by the gentleman in the green coat was later replaced by a plain linen 'stock' or neck-cloth.

Ladies began to wear their hair dressed high, and by George III's reign, which began in 1760, it was worn very high indeed. It was pinned over horsehair pads, then greased heavily and powdered with flour. It may have looked grand, but it does not seem to have been a very clean fashion. If a lady was caught in the rain the flour and grease in her hair turned into sticky dough!

Men's wigs were powdered, too, and their clothes were very elegant and expensive. The sedan chair you see in the picture was a popular way of getting about in town.

The Regency

The last part of the Georgian period is called the Regency, because in 1811 the Prince of Wales became Regent, ruling for his father who was ill. It was the time of Beau Brummell, a friend of the Prince Regent and the leader of men's fashions between 1798 and 1816.

Beau Brummell's influence on men's clothes was enormous. He made people pay very particular attention to the quality and tailoring of their clothes, and he set new standards of taste. This was, of course, only among the very rich, but everyone tried to follow the lead.

It was partly owing to Beau Brummell's influence that people stopped greasing and powdering their hair, and washed it instead. It was no longer necessary to use strong scent to drown the smell of unwashed clothes and bodies.

The picture shows some important passengers travelling to India on an East India Merchantman. The very tight trousers the gentleman is wearing are called 'pantaloons'. His coat is cut away in front to show his splendid waistcoat, and has tails at the back, like modern full evening dress. He is talking to another passenger also dressed in the fashion of the period.

The Days of the Stage Coach

The picture shows a stage coach which has stopped at an inn to change horses. It is about the year 1830 and by this time men's clothes had become more like the ones worn to-day.

Men wore trousers, waistcoats and coats, though the coats were longer and fuller. A stock was worn wrapped round the throat.

Ladies had tiny waists and wore very full skirts, very full 'leg o' mutton' sleeves and pretty bonnets. In cold weather they carried muffs to keep their hands warm. Little girls wore long, white 'pantalettes', edged with lace, under their skirts.

Two inventions of this period were patent leather for shoes and belts, and a waterproof cloth, patented by Mr. Charles Mackintosh, from which came the word mackintosh. High boots of one type were called Wellington boots, after the great Duke of Wellington.

The coachman in the picture is wearing a coat with capes. This was a fashion of thirty years before, but everyone did not give up a good garment because the fashion changed. The capes kept the shoulders dry, an important advantage when driving a four-in-hand in heavy rain.

The Early Days of the Railway

In the early years of Queen Victoria's long reign (1837—1901), life in Britain changed in many ways. Factories were built, new machinery was installed, towns grew rapidly, people moved from the country to the towns, and the railways spread across the land. People could earn more money, and more people could afford good clothes.

Men's clothes became sober and the bright colours of older days went out of use, except for soldiers. The picture shows a railway station in about 1860, with a number of examples of the fashions. The top hat was still the usual wear for men, but the curly 'bowler' began to be used as well. Men began to wear whiskers; beards, long moustaches and curly side-whiskers were common. Trousers were strapped under the boots.

The new idea for ladies was the crinoline, a skirt worn over a frame made of whalebone, bamboo or wire. This looked very elegant, but think how much room it would take up in a crowded railway carriage!

Although there were more people with money, there were still very many who had to do the best they could with plain, unfashionable hard-wearing clothes.

Victorian Country Scene

Country people did not follow changing fashion as much as townsfolk. The farmer was often rather old-fashioned, but insisted on good quality for hard wear. His wife naturally liked to be as up-to-date as possible, but she usually made her own gowns and dresses at home, buying the material from the market town.

The farmer in the picture, which could be in the middle of the Victorian age, perhaps about 1870, wears a long, loose jacket of very good quality. He wears breeches and yellow gaiters over his strong boots. The hard-crowned brown hat was popular for a long time.

The farmer's wife wears her home-made gown and a shawl over her shoulders. Her hair is in ringlets which show under her bonnet.

The carter wears a smock, which was almost universal in the country in those days for farm workers. Each county had its own colour, and its own pattern of embroidery. The linen was often spun and woven at home, and then embroidered, or 'smocked', in the traditional way. A countryman would never dream of wearing the smock of another county.

Late Victorian

Our picture shows a family party at the theatre about the year 1890—a period called the 'Gay Nineties'. They are wearing their best clothes for the occasion.

The lady wears a 'bustle', which came into fashion when the crinoline went out. The back of the skirt is padded and bunched up, and decorated with roses. The waist is small, and to achieve this, she wears very tight corsets underneath. Her hair is piled high with a flower decoration.

Father is in full evening dress, which is not very different from to-day. His son is wearing a sailor suit, and he will have a wooden whistle on a white lanyard in his pocket. Little boys sometimes wore velvet suits with lace collars, and long, curly hair for boys and girls was much admired.

His sister wears a frilly dress and gloves like her mother. The velvet band round her hair is pretty, and girls sometimes wear one to-day.

Children's clothes were still formal and fussy. For daily wear boys wore knickerbockers with long, black stockings over their knees. Girls wore long stockings, too, and rather elaborate frocks.

The Edwardians

Queen Victoria was succeeded in 1901 by King Edward VII, and his reign—which lasted until 1910—gave the name to the Edwardian period and Edwardian fashions. The clothes and bathing costumes in the picture may look funny to us, but at the time they were up-to-date and very fashionable.

The bathing costumes were much more complicated than they are to-day and not, one might think, very good for swimming. People changed in bathing machines, small dressing rooms on wheels which were pulled right down to the edge of the sea by horses. Everything had to be very private.

The gentleman on the beach is wearing the correct sea side clothes of the period, a striped blazer with tie and hat-band to match. His straw hat was called a 'boater'. The lady is wearing a typical dress of the Edwardian days. It is shapely, with a long skirt and a wide belt. The hat is wide-brimmed and elegant and she has a parasol.

Seaside holidays were becoming increasingly popular, and more and more people began to feel they could afford the benefits and pleasures of an annual holiday.

Edwardian Motoring

With the Edwardian age came the first motor cars and the earliest aeroplanes. If you were lucky enough to go motoring you wore special clothes, because cars were open and the roads were very dusty. The owner of the car in the picture wears a heavy overcoat and a cap and goggles.

The lady is well wrapped up, too, and her hat is secured with a scarf tied under her chin. Often ladies protected their faces with motoring veils.

The gentleman watching the car being started is wearing a tweed suit of the style popular for week-ends or holidays. He is also wearing a straw hat. For business he would dress more formally in black coat and striped trousers, and probably a top hat. Men wore stiff collars in town and country.

The soldier in the picture is wearing a scarlet tunic and 'pill-box' hat. A smart moustache was popular then. Horses were still in general use for wagons, carriages or cabs, like the Hansom cab in the picture. The motor car was noisy, smelly and not very reliable, and remained a novelty for some time.

The End of an Age

In 1914 a terrible war broke out, which we call World War I, and when it ended in 1918 nothing was quite the same. The people watching the procession in 1913 belong to an age which was soon to end.

The gentleman on the balcony is in 'morning dress', which is the same as men wear to-day on very special occasions. In those days it was normal dress for everyday for nearly all professional and business men. The lady has an elegant dress and a splendid hat with feathers and wings. Their little boy wears an 'Eton jacket' and an 'Eton collar', worn by all well-to-do schoolboys.

The gentleman on the steps is in a 'lounge suit' which had come into general use, and he wears a straw hat. The suit is very much the same as people wear to-day, but he has a stiff shirt collar and cuffs. The gentleman with his hands in his pockets has a gold watch-chain, which nearly every man wore across his waistcoat.

The difference between the rich and the poor still showed in the clothes they wore, but that was soon to disappear.

The 'Twenties

The picture shows a group of passengers waiting to take their places in one of the early air-liners about 1925. Here is a great change in dress from the previous picture.

The ladies are wearing short skirts, nearly to the knees, and silk stockings. The lady without a hat has her hair cut as short as a man's—this was called an 'Eton crop'. One of the ladies is smoking a cigarette in public, which would have been very shocking ten years before. One lady wears a 'cloche hat' and the other a bandeau, which is a scarf tied tightly round her head. Most of the dresses at this time had no waist at all.

The men's clothes are not very different from to-day, except for the man wearing very wide trousers which were known as 'Oxford bags'. The baggy breeches are 'Plus fours' designed for golf, but popular for leisure wear.

During the next forty years dress became more sensible. Men gave up always wearing a waistcoat, and either went without or wore a jersey or a cardigan. Men and women began to go about without hats, and women sometimes used head-scarves. For formal occasions, however, there has been little change.

Clothes of To-day

The main characteristics of modern dress are comfort and good colours. The family in the picture shows how easy and gay the clothes are. Father's jersey and scarf are essentially comfortable, though if he works in an office in the city he may go off in the morning in a black coat and waistcoat, black shoes and a bowler hat—and carry an umbrella.

Mother wears trousers, which would have shocked her grandparents in their day. They are comfortable, easier for casual wear than a skirt, and also very smart.

The greatest change generally is in children's clothes. Once they were stuffy and stiff for boys and frilly for girls; now they are gay and designed for free movement.

The boy wears 'jeans', worn these days by boys and girls, young and old. For school he probably wears shorts and a blazer, or perhaps a jersey like his father is wearing.

The little boy wears easy and brightly coloured clothes and no socks; not very long ago children always wore socks or, when they were older, stockings.

If you look back through this book you will see that we are dressing more like people in the earliest ages, instead of using clothes as a kind of ornamentation we wear them for their real purpose, to keep warm and to be comfortable.

Roman soldier

Norman soldier

Medieval

Medieval workman

Tudor

Cavalier

Puritan

William and Mary

Georgian

Regency

Early Victorian

Late Victorian